von Wolfgang Hamm

15-Minuten-Tests
Englisch Klasse 5/6

Ernst Klett Schulbuchverlag
Stuttgart · Leipzig

Inhaltsverzeichnis

Bildquellen:
Cover: shutterstock (RF/JoLin); **2.1** Fotolia.com (iconshow), New York; **4.1** shutterstock (Anastasiia Kucherenko), New York, NY; **7.1** Fotolia.com (Sylverarts), New York; **7.2** Thinkstock (Stockbyte), München; **10.1** Fotolia.com (lesniewski), New York; **12.1** dreamstime.com (Paulo Alejandro Gomez), Brentwood, TN; **13.2** MEV Verlag GmbH, Augsburg; **15.1** shutterstock (archana bhartia), New York, NY; **16.2** dreamstime.com (Zhouzheng), Brentwood, TN; **17.1** dreamstime.com (Biserko), Brentwood, TN; **20.1** Thinkstock (Digital Vision), München; **21.2** CC-BY-3.0 (Mitchazenia), siehe *1; **26.1** dreamstime.com (Binkski), Brentwood, TN; **26.2** Nationales Olympisches Komitee für Deutschland, Frankfurt am Main; **30.1** Fotolia.com (AST), New York; **31.2** Fotolia.com (dario), New York; **31.3** Thinkstock (iStockphoto), München; **31.5** Fotolia.com (dario), New York; **35.2** Thinkstock (Hemera), München; **35.3** dreamstime.com (Ruthrgb), Brentwood, TN; **35.4** Thinkstock (iStockphoto), München; **36.2** shutterstock (olegtoka), New York, NY; **36.3** Fotolia.com (OrpheusXL), New York; **39.1** Fotolia.com (Brux), New York; **42.2** shutterstock (Anton Brand), New York, NY

1. Auflage

1 6 5 4 3 2 1 | 2017 2016 2015 2014 2013

Internetadresse: www.klett.de
Autor: Wolfgang Hamm, Marktredwitz
Redaktion: Elisabeth Schneeweiss-Bauer
Umschlag- und Layoutgestaltung: Susanne Fiedler
Reproduktion: Meyle + Müller, Medien-Management, Pforzheim
Druck: Medienhaus Plump GmbH, Rheinbreitbach
Printed in Germany
ISBN 978-3-12-547487-1

9 783125 474871

Liebe Schülerin, lieber Schüler,

jeder der 15-Minuten-Tests besteht aus 16–17 Fragen mit vier möglichen Antworten. Die Antworten müssen in der Regel nur angekreuzt werden. Manchmal muss auch ein Wort eingesetzt werden. Die Aufgabenstellung ist absichtlich unterschiedlich gestellt, so dass du manchmal das Richtige, manchmal aber auch das Falsche von den vier Möglichkeiten herausfinden musst. Daher solltest du die Arbeitsanweisungen ganz genau lesen!

Diese Tests sind für 5. und 6. Klassen aller Schularten gedacht. Du kannst sie zu Hause als unterhaltsame Erweiterung deiner sprachlichen Fähigkeiten einsetzen, als Übungsmaterial zur Gewöhnung an zunehmend standardisierte Testformen, zur Abwechslung im Schulalltag, um Zwischenbilanz zu ziehen.
Für jeden Test sollten etwa 15 Minuten eingeplant werden. Diese Testform wird zunehmend in der Schule und bei Bewerbungen eingesetzt. Auch dort hast du für die Bearbeitung nur begrenzt Zeit. Halte dich daher nicht zu lange an Aufgaben auf, die du nicht auf Anhieb verstehst. Hab' auch Mut, Lösungen zu erraten.
Wer nichts ankreuzt, bekommt auf jeden Fall keinen Punkt.
Die Tests folgen einer Progression, d. h. die leichteren Tests stehen am Anfang, nach hinten wird es immer ein bisschen schwieriger.

Deinen bearbeiteten Test kannst du selbst kontrollieren, indem du im Lösungsteil die richtigen Antworten mit deinen Antworten vergleichst. Am Ende des Buches kannst du die erreichte Punktzahl in eine Tabelle eintragen und hast so einen Überblick über deinen Lernerfolg.
Mit jedem Test wird *Learning by testing* praktiziert, d. h. die konzentrierte Durchführung der Tests mit ihren unterschiedlichen Fragestellungen schult dein Sprachverständnis und erweitert deine Kenntnisse im Englischen in so wichtigen Bereichen wie Vokabular, Grammatik, Leseverstehen, Kommunikation, Landeskunde, Aussprache und Rechtschreibung.
Das sollte dir eine Viertelstunde wert sein! Viel Spaß beim Testen.

Los geht's mit Test 1!

Vocabulary

1 Put the words in the right alphabetical order. Use numbers.

a) ____ homework
b) ____ school
c) ____ teacher
d) ____ classroom

2 Which spelling is not correct? Tick it (✓).

a) Wednesday ☐
b) Thuesday ☐
c) Thursday ☐
d) Friday ☐

3 One word doesn't fit.

a) great ☐
b) boring ☐
c) good ☐
d) beautiful ☐

4 Which pair is wrong?

a) apple and pie ☐
b) fish and chips ☐
c) pen and book ☐
d) bacon and eggs ☐

5 Complete the sentences. One word doesn't fit.

go • play • read • ride • do

a) You can __________ a bike.
b) You can __________ an exercise.
c) You can __________ the guitar.
d) You can __________ comics.

6 **Which two words don't rhyme?**

a) send – friend ☐
b) like – bike ☐
c) tea – my ☐
d) make – cake ☐

Communication

7 **Draw smileys:** ☺ ☹

a) "You're cool." ◯
b) "That's nice." ◯
c) "Sorry, you're wrong." ◯
d) "OK great!" ◯

8 **Put the dialogue in the correct order. Use numbers.**

a) ____ "Good idea. Let's meet at 7 o'clock."
b) ____ "Can we go swimming on Saturday?"
c) ____ "Bye."
d) ____ "Oh, no! Let's go to the cinema."

Grammar

9 **Which article is wrong?**

a) *an* apple ☐
b) *an* exercise book ☐
c) *an* uniform ☐
d) *an* English book ☐

10 **Which sentence is wrong?**

a) *There's* a sandwich on the table. ☐
b) *There are* some crisps in the school bag. ☐
c) *There's* a hamburger under the desk. ☐
d) *There are* some chocolate on the desk. ☐

11 **Complete the sentences. One pronoun doesn't fit.**

my • your • her • our • their

a) Linda: "Let's look at some of ____________ photos, Lucy. Who's that?"
b) Lucy: "That's Carol Brown. She's a friend from ______________ old school."
c) Lucy: "The Browns have got a new house and ___________ garden is big."
d) Linda: "Yes, but ____________ garden is nicer."

12 **Which long form is not correct? <u>Underline</u> it.**

a) Sally: "I'm new in Greenwich." → I am
b) Tom and Ken: "We aren't at Thomas Tallis." → are not
c) Mary: "Look, that's Sally over there." → that is
d) Mary: "She's got two young cats." → She is

Reading

13 **Read these four sentences and find the correct logical order. Use numbers.**

a) ____ They give her a present.
b) ____ It's a pair of sunglasses.
c) ____ Tracy's friends all come to her birthday party.
d) ____ She opens the box.

14 **Where do you find this sign?**

DON'T COME INTO MY ROOM.

a) at school ☐
b) at home ☐
c) on a farm ☐
d) in a department store ☐

Culture

15 **. . . is not a sight in London.**

a) Tower Bridge ☐
b) The White House ☐
c) The Houses of Parliament ☐
d) Buckingham Palace ☐

16 Which statements are right?

Big Ben …

a) is over a thousand years old. ☐
b) is a famous clock in London. ☐
c) is in Paris. ☐
d) weighs 13,200 kilos. ☐

17 Which statement is wrong?

a) London's taxis are yellow. ☐
b) A lot of London's buses are red. ☐
c) The London Underground is called the 'Tube'. ☐
d) Queen Elizabeth lives in Buckingham Palace. ☐

Vocabulary

1 Put the words in the right alphabetical order. Use numbers.

a) ____ bed
b) ____ birthday
c) ____ bike
d) ____ badminton

2 Find the word with a spelling mistake.

a) four ☐
b) fourteen ☐
c) fourty ☐
d) forty-four ☐

3 You can only tidy *(clean)* . . .

a) a living room. ☐
b) a book. ☐
c) a person. ☐
d) a cake. ☐

4 Which pair is wrong?

a) good and bad ☐
b) left and write ☐
c) young and old ☐
d) big and small ☐

5 Which word doesn't fit?

do • make • put • clean • take

a) Please ______________ a photo of our cat.
b) Please ______________ the books on the shelf.
c) You must ______________ your homework now.
d) Why did you ______________ so many mistakes?

6 **Which two words don't rhyme?**

a) wait - white ☐
b) all - small ☐
c) bed - head ☐
d) there - wear ☐

Communication

7 **Which answer is wrong?**

"Can I have your pen?"
a) "Sorry, I need it." ☐
b) "Yes, of course." ☐
c) "Please." ☐
d) "Sure." ☐

8 **What is the correct order? Use numbers.**

a) ____ A quiz show, I think.
b) ____ But I love them.
c) ____ What's on television today?
d) ____ Oh, no, not again. I don't like quiz shows.

Grammar

9 **Which plural form is wrong?**

a) pen → pens ☐
b) baby → babys ☐
c) sandwich → sandwiches ☐
d) story → stories ☐

10 **Which s-genitive is wrong?**

a) Our cat's name is Tiger. ☐
b) Lisa is Ronas sister. ☐
c) Tom is Mark's brother. ☐
d) The Spencers' new flat is in Oxford Street. ☐

11 **Complete each sentence with the correct pronoun. One doesn't fit.**

me • him • her • our • them

a) "Where's Linda? I can't see __________."
b) "My parents? Let's ask __________."
c) "Tom is here. You can talk to __________ now."
d) "Show __________ the way, please."

12 **Which imperative is wrong?**

a) *Don't write* in your English books. ☐
b) *Open* your books, please. ☐
c) Please *are* quiet. ☐
d) Please *don't call* Evelyn now. ☐

Reading

13 **Read these four sentences. What's the correct order? Use numbers.**

a) ____ In the evening, Emma takes her dog for a walk.
b ____ She always goes to bed at 9 p.m.
c) ____ After school, at about 4 p.m. Emma often plays the guitar.
d) ____ Then she does her homework.

14 **What does this sign mean?**

KIDS GO FREE!

Children ...
a) are alone. ☐
b) don't have to pay. ☐
c) have no parents. ☐
d) can use the playground. ☐

Culture

15 Where does Halloween come from?

a) Asia ☐
b) France ☐
c) the USA ☐
d) Germany ☐

16 When is Valentine's Day? In ...

a) February. ☐
b) June. ☐
c) August. ☐
d) October. ☐

17 Tick (✓) the right person who you send a Valentine card to.

a) your doctor ☐
b) your friend ☐
c) your teacher ☐
d) your grandad ☐

Vocabulary

1 Put the words in the right alphabetical order. Use numbers.

a) ____ more
b) ____ mouth
c) ____ mouse
d) ____ Monday

2 Find the word with a spelling mistake.

a) spring ☐
b) summer ☐
c) autum ☐
d) winter ☐

3 Which of these things isn't on a shopping list?

a) a bag of apples ☐
b) a part of a story ☐
c) a bottle of milk ☐
d) a box of eggs ☐

4 Which phrase is wrong?

a) a bar of crisps ☐
b) a bottle of lemonade ☐
c) a box of eggs ☐
d) a packet of biscuits ☐

5 Complete the sentences. One verb doesn't fit.

say • speak • spell • talk • tell

a) Can you ________________ me the way to the station?
b) Sorry, I can't ________________ your name. It's too difficult.
c) Never forget to ________________ 'Please' and 'Thank you'.
d) Can you ________________ French?

6 Which two words don't rhyme?

a) when – again ☐
b) even – seven ☐
c) sea – me ☐
d) one – run ☐

Communication

7 Draw smileys: ☺ ☹

a) "Oh, I'm sorry." ◯
b) "Your jokes are boring!" ◯
c) "That's no problem." ◯
d) "Very nice." ◯

8 Which answer is correct?

"How are you?"
a) "I'm ten." ☐
b) "Thank you, I'm fine." ☐
c) "How do you do?" ☐
d) "Bye." ☐

Grammar

9 Which verb form is correct?

Emma … to the Drama Club every week.
a) go ☐
b) gos ☐
c) goes ☐
d) going ☐

10 Which verb form is correct?

We … go to school on Sundays.
a) do ☐
b) does ☐
c) don't ☐
d) doesn't ☐

11 Which short answer is correct?

Can you hire bikes in Greenwich Park? – No, you …

a) aren't. ☐
b) can. ☐
c) don't. ☐
d) can't. ☐

12 Which question is correct?

… you … the answer?

a) Do … know … ☐
b) Do … knows … ☐
c) Does … know … ☐
d) Does … knows … ☐

Reading

Read this poster and answer the questions.

13 Which statement is wrong?

You go to the Drama Club if you are good at …

a) singing. ☐
b) dancing. ☐
c) playing a musical instrument. ☐
d) singing and dancing. ☐

14 Which statement is correct?

You will become an actor/actress if you …

a) go to the Club every weekend. ☐
b) meet your friends after school. ☐
c) have time after school on Tuesdays. ☐
d) phone Mrs Lansky. ☐

DRAMA CLUB?
WHAT ABOUT YOU?

Can you sing? – Good!
Can you dance? – Great!
Can you sing and dance? – Fantastic!
We've got the right thing for you!

We meet in the hall every Tuesday at 4.30 p.m.
Ask Mrs Lansky.

Culture

15 Which country is not a part of Great Britain?

a) England ☐
b) Wales ☐
c) Scotland ☐
d) Ireland ☐

16 Which statement is wrong?

a) England is part of the United Kingdom. ☐
b) Its currency is the pound: £. ☐
c) England isn't part of the European Community. ☐
d) England belongs to the European Community. ☐

17 Which answer is right?

Between Britain and the rest of Europe is …

a) the Pacific Ocean. ☐
b) the North Sea. ☐
c) the Indian Ocean. ☐
d) the Thames. ☐

Vocabulary

1 Put the words in the right alphabetical order. Use numbers.

a) ____ cousin
b) ____ count
c) ____ country
d) ____ colour

2 Capital letters: Find the word with a spelling mistake.

a) Mustafa's favourite food is Turkish. ☐
b) "Did you watch TV last Saturday, Tim?" ☐
c) Last weekend Terry went to the london Eye. ☐
d) "Look, Emma and I are drawing a ship." ☐

3 What don't you have for breakfast in England?

a) bacon and eggs ☐
b) fish and chips ☐
c) tea ☐
d) sausages ☐

4 Which pair is wrong?

a) bike and helmet ☐
b) teacher and rain ☐
c) present and past ☐
d) alarm and clock ☐

5 Complete the sentences. One verb doesn't fit.

answer • ask • call • cry • shout

a) Do you think we should ______________ the police?
b) Did Teresa ______________ for help?
c) Sandy was unhappy, but she didn't ______________.
d) ______________ your teacher if you have a question.

6 **Which two words don't rhyme?**

a) know – now ☐
b) and – hand ☐
c) guitar – are ☐
d) late – great ☐

Communication

7 **Put the sentences in the right order. Use numbers.**

a) ____ Thank you.
b) ____ Can you tell me the time, please?
c) ____ No problem.
d) ____ Yes, of course. It's a quarter past six.

8 **Complete the sentences. One word doesn't fit.**

not far • straight • excuse • come • get

a) ______________ me, please. Is there a snack bar near here?
b) Yes, there's one ______________ from here.
c) How do I ______________ there?
d) First go ______________ on. Then turn right. The snack bar is on the left.

Grammar

9 **Which date is wrong?**

a) 2nd June → the twenty-second of June ☐
b) 5th Feb. → the fifth of February ☐
c) 12th Jan. → the twelfth of January ☐
d) 3rd April → the third of April ☐

10 **Word order: Which sentence is wrong?**

a) I sometimes meet my friends at the weekend. ☐
b) You always come to school late. ☐
c) I eat often pizza. ☐
d) We never play rugby in the street. ☐

11 Which sentence is correct?

a) Can you please Jade help, Hannah. ☐
b) Terry, you cann't play football in your room. ☐
c) Sam can the best sandwiches make. ☐
d) Lisa can't do her Maths homework. ☐

12 Which word is spelled correctly?

Ashton often … his room on Saturday morning.

a) tidy ☐
b) tidis ☐
c) tidies ☐
d) tidys ☐

Reading

Read this poster and answer the questions.

13 Which statement is correct?

a) It's a special offer for kids. ☐
b) You'll go from Paris to London. ☐
c) You'll go from London to Paris. ☐
d) You spend three days in France. ☐

14 Which of these statements is not in the text?

The offer …

a) is for the autumn months. ☐
b) is for the new Disneyland Hotel. ☐
c) is a good price. ☐
d) is all inclusive. ☐

ETA
(THE EXPLORER TRAVEL AGENCY) LONDON OFFERS:

ENJOY
DISNEYLAND PARIS/FRANCE
AND STAY AT THE
NEW DISNEYLAND HOTEL.

3 NIGHTS
FROM £ 199

(SEPTEMBER – NOVEMBER)

Culture

15 The ... is between France and England.

a) M1 motorway ☐
b) Channel Tunnel ☐
c) Route 66 ☐
d) Downing Street ☐

16 Which statement is wrong?

Scotland is famous for ...

a) bagpipes. ☐
b) oil in the North Sea. ☐
c) the Cutty Sark. ☐
d) Loch Ness. ☐

17 All these are English counties, except ...

a) Cornwall. ☐
b) Devon. ☐
c) Wales. ☐
d) Yorkshire. ☐

Vocabulary

1 **Put the words in the right alphabetical order. Use numbers.**

a) ____ miss
b) ____ milk
c) ____ million
d) ____ minute

2 **Which letters don't you hear? Underline them.**
(Example: is̲land)

a) write
b) talk
c) listen
d) knife

3 **... isn't a school subject.**

a) Technology ☐
b) Science Fiction ☐
c) Geography ☐
d) History ☐

4 **Which pair is wrong?**

a) easy – difficult ☐
b) sunny – rainy ☐
c) warm – boring ☐
d) quick – slow ☐

5 **Complete the sentences. One verb doesn't fit.**

bring • carry • move • take • wear

a) Your bag looks heavy. Can I ________________ it for you?
b) Does Carol always ________________ jeans and T-shirts?
c) Can you ________________ me that knife, Tim?
d) Please ________________ that book to the library on the first floor.

6 **Which two words don't rhyme?**

a) go - show ☐
b) sing - bring ☐
c) straight - street ☐
d) pound - sound ☐

Communication

7 **Put the sentences in the right order. Use numbers.**

a) ____ But what about that new game show?
b) ____ What's on TV today?
c) ____ Well, it's quite funny. Let's watch it together.
d) ____ Nothing interesting.

8 **Complete the sentences. One word doesn't fit.**

because • *instead of* • *or* • *for* • *at*

a) Why can't I have pizza __________ dinner?
b) You can't have it __________ you need something different every day.
c) Do you mean a cheese pizza __________ a vegetarian pizza?
d) No, I mean salad __________ a pizza.

Grammar

9 **Which spelling is wrong?**

a) 20th July → the twentyth of July ☐
b) 6th Sept. → the sixth of September ☐
c) 15th March → the fifteenth of March ☐
d) 31st Dec. → the thirty-first of December ☐

10 **Which is correct?**

… Nella always … to Greenwich by bus?

a) Does … goes ☐
b) Do … go ☐
c) Does … go ☐
d) Do … goes ☐

11 **Which is correct?**

… … Lisa to school? – Her mum.

a) Who takes … ☐
b) Who does take … ☐
c) Who take … ☐
d) Who do takes … ☐

12 **Which adverb is usually not used with the -ing form?**

a) now ☐
b) always ☐
c) just ☐
d) still ☐

Reading

Read this report from a school magazine and answer the questions.

THE QUEEN'S VISIT TO EXETER

What a day to remember! On Wednesday, 2nd May 2012, some pupils at St. Margaret's School in Exeter had the chance to meet Her Majesty the Queen and her husband, the Duke of Edinburgh, in Exeter.

One of them, Rebecca, wrote this report:

At about 4 p.m. we all headed down to the Cathedral Yard to see the Queen for her Diamond Jubilee* visit. While we were waiting for the Queen, we waved our flags. When the Queen arrived, Sylvie, Mark, Toby, Carol and I went to the Queen and Prince Philip and talked with them! We took four corgis with us and the Queen and Prince Philip commented on them!
When I got home that night, my mum showed me a couple of websites and to my surprise I saw Sylvie's and my feet with the corgis. Now our feet are famous!

* Diamond Jubilee – sechzigjähriges Jubiläum als Königin

13 **Which of these statements is correct?**

The Queen and the Duke of Edinburgh ...

a) celebrated their Diamond Jubilee in 2012. ☐
b) visited St Margaret's School in Exeter. ☐
c) had four corgis with them. ☐
d) visited the Cathedral in Exeter. ☐

14 **Which of these statements is wrong?**

The pupils were surprised that ...

a) they could talk with the Queen and her husband. ☐
b) the Queen and her husband spoke about the corgis. ☐
c) Rebecca's mum wanted to take some photos. ☐
d) the photos on the Internet showed their feet. ☐

Culture

15 **Which statement is wrong?**

a) The Thames is a river. ☐
b) Ben Nevis is a mountain. ☐
c) Loch Ness is a monster. ☐
d) Edinburgh is a city. ☐

16 **The Meridian Line goes through ...**

a) Cambridge. ☐
b) Oxford. ☐
c) Greenwich. ☐
d) Plymouth. ☐

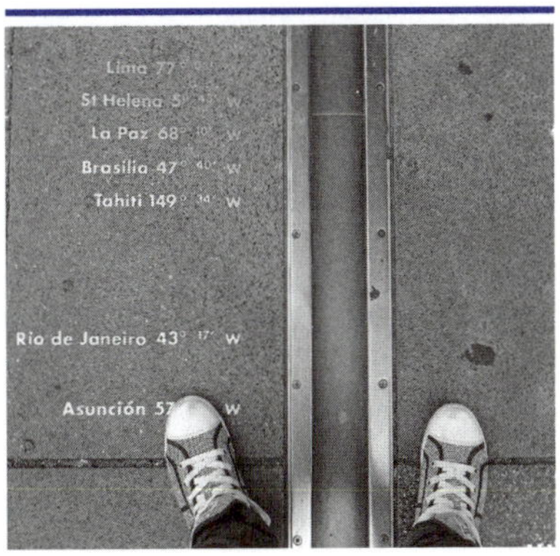

17 **Which of these aren't British meals?**

a) fish and chips ☐
b) chicken curry ☐
c) pizza ☐
d) apple pie ☐

Vocabulary

1 Which of these four examples doesn't show the word 'pocket money'?

a) NEYTOCEKMOP ☐

b) ['pɒkɪt ˌmʌni] ☐

c) YƎNOM TƎꓘƆOꟼ ☐

d) TOPMAYKOCEN ☐

2 Which letters don't you hear? Underline them.

a) climb
b) know
c) walk
d) wrong

3 You don't do this at a party:

a) sing karaoke ☐
b) learn English ☐
c) dance ☐
d) listen to music ☐

4 Which pair is wrong?

a) letter + box ☐
b) book + shop ☐
c) table + fork ☐
d) play + ground ☐

5 Complete the sentences. One word doesn't fit.

also • although • because • then • or

a) I can't go to your party ______________ I'm ill.
b) I think there were twenty ______________ thirty pupils in the classroom.
c) Carol often cycles fast ______________ she knows it's dangerous.
d) Tina is hungry and she's ______________ very tired.

6 Which two words don't rhyme?

a) steak - brake ☐
b) bought - boat ☐
c) fight - white ☐
d) tin - begin ☐

Communication

7 Read the German sentences and number the correct English translations. There's an example (0) for you.

0	Wie alt bist du?
1	Wie geht es dir?
2	Woher kommst du?
3	Wie viel muss ich dafür zahlen?
4	Wie viele CDs hast du?
5	Wie wäre es mit Freitag um 7?
6	Was kosten die Postkarten?

	How about Friday at 7?
	How much must I pay?
	How much are the postcards?
	Where are you from?
0	How old are you?
	How many CDs do you have?
	How are you?

Grammar

8 Which verb in the present progressive form is not spelled correctly?

a) It's raining and I'm getting wet. ☐
b) Ron is phoneing. ☐
c) We're shopping. ☐
d) She's making tea. ☐

9 **Use the correct form of 'to be'.**

'm • 's • 're • isn't • aren't

a) Where is little Brittney? Why __________ she playing with the others?
b) Oh, no, it __________ snowing again.
c) I __________ meeting Tyler on Sunday.
d) We __________ watching DVDs after school.

10 **On the phone. Use the correct question word and complete the sentences.**

what • when • where • how • who

a) ______________ am I talking to?
b) ______________ are you watching on TV at the moment? A soap or the news?
c) ______________ are we going to the beach? By car or by bus?
d) ______________ are you going shopping? At Marks and Spencer or at Harrods?

11 **Which possessive pronoun is wrong?**

a) Whose dog is in our garden? – It's Cathy's. It's *her* dog. ☐
b) Is this your bike? – Yes, it's *his* bike. ☐
c) Are those your skateboards? – Yes, these are *our* skateboards. ☐
d) Whose shoes are these? – They are Nick's and David's. They are *their* shoes. ☐

12 **Mark the wrong word: 'some' or 'any'?**

a) Brendan wants to buy some chocolate. ☐
b) Michael doesn't have some pocket money left. ☐
c) Is there any milk in the fridge? ☐
d) Ryan doesn't want any coffee. ☐

Reading

Read this notice and answer the questions.

13 Which statement is not in the text?

a) If you are interested in drama, you should see Mrs Williams next week. ☐
b) Girls and boys of all ages can take part. ☐
c) The rehearsals* will start in February. ☐
d) The audition doesn't begin before lunch. ☐

* Proben

CIRENCESTER KINGSHILL SCHOOL
KINGSHILL LANE
CIRENCESTER, GLOUCESTERSHIRE GL7 1HS, UNITED KINGDOM

TODAY: JANUARY 10TH, 2013
ZARA WILLIAMS, ROOM 102

14 Which statement is wrong?

a) You needn't go in. ☐
b) You shouldn't go in. ☐
c) You should stay outside. ☐
d) You mustn't go in. ☐

DO NOT ENTER

Culture

15 Jamie Oliver is a famous British . . .

a) artist. ☐
b) cook. ☐
c) singer. ☐
d) football player. ☐

16 Which statement is true?

Justin Bieber was born in ….
a) England. ☐
b) America. ☐
c) Canada. ☐
d) Ireland. ☐

17 Which statement is wrong?

a) Mr Bean (Rowan Atkinson) – comedian ☐
b) Robbie Williams – singer ☐
c) Harry Potter – a person in a book / film ☐
d) James Bond – football player ☐

Vocabulary

1 Which of these four examples shows the word 'surprise'?

a) RISURAPS ☐

b) [sə'praɪθ] ☐

c) ᗡƎƧIЯꟼЯUƧ ☐

d) PURRIESS ☐

2 Which words do you pronounce [raɪt]?

a) right ☐
b) ride ☐
c) write ☐
d) white ☐

3 Which phrase is wrong?

a) take pictures ☐
b) get lost ☐
c) eat down ☐
d) turn off ☐

4 Opposites: One pair is wrong.

a) now – at the moment ☐
b) tomorrow – yesterday ☐
c) a long time ago – next year ☐
d) this evening – this morning ☐

5 Which two words don't rhyme?

a) toe – slow ☐
b) nose – north ☐
c) red – said ☐
d) ring – king ☐

Communication

6 **Read the German sentences and number the correct English translations. There's an example (0) for you.**

0	Wie alt bist du?
1	Wie ist das Wetter heute?
2	Welche Jahreszeit magst du am liebsten?
3	Heute regnet es überall.
4	Wo ist es oft sonnig und warm?
5	Welchen Monat magst du nicht?
6	Ich liebe den Monat Mai.

	Where is it often sunny and hot?
	I love the month of May.
	Which month don't you like?
	What's your favourite season?
	What's the weather like today?
0	How old are you?
	It's raining everywhere today.

Grammar

7 **Which adverb is usually not used with the simple past?**

a) already ☐
b) yesterday ☐
c) ago ☐
d) last ☐

8 **Which form of 'to be' is not correct?**

a) We *were* all in Year 6 last year. ☐
b) *Were* you at home in July? ☐
c) I *was* in Scotland in the summer. ☐
d) Yesterday it *were* hot and sunny. ☐

9 Which verb has got the wrong irregular past forms?

a) get – got – got ☐
b) know – knowed – known ☐
c) go – went – gone ☐
d) do – did – done ☐

10 Which verb is not spelled correctly?

a) stay → staied ☐
b) carry → carried ☐
c) stop → stopped ☐
d) invite → invited ☐

11 Which form is correct?

I … to assembly last Monday.

a) don't go ☐
b) didn't went ☐
c) don't went ☐
d) didn't go ☐

Reading

Read this text message.

Hi Kenny,
How was your trip to the LONDON EYE 2day?
Did you have fun? I'm having a gr8 time in town. Do you want to come over l8r?
Meet at Trafalgar Sq.?
CU K8

12 Which statement is wrong?

a) Kate is sending Kenny a message. ☐
b) Kate saw the LONDON EYE today. ☐
c) She wants to meet Kenny. ☐
d) The meeting point is: Trafalgar Square in London. ☐

Read this poem.

> I am an *'A'.*
> Born in *August,*
> Sometimes *angry,*
> I don't like *alarm clocks* or *awful aunts.*
> I like *animals*
> and *Arsenal,*
> And in *autumn*
> I eat a lot of *apples.*
> But being *alone*
> Is not *always* fun.
> I am an *'A'.*

13 Which statement is wrong?

The writer of this poem …

a) likes to be with his / her friends. ☐
b) always celebrates his / her birthday in the summer. ☐
c) likes to get up early. ☐
d) is a fan of a London football club. ☐

Culture

14 The Olympic Games in 2012 took place in . . .

a) Athens, Greece. ☐
b) London, England. ☐
c) Rio, Brazil. ☐
d) Sydney, Australia. ☐

15 Which isn't a famous English football club?

a) Chelsea ☐
b) Wimbledon ☐
c) Manchester United ☐
d) Arsenal ☐

16 Many sports have their origins in England except . . .

a) tennis. ☐
b) badminton. ☐
c) handball. ☐
d) rugby. ☐

Vocabulary

1 Which of these four examples doesn't show the word 'language'?

a) GAULAGEN ☐

b) ['læŋgwɪdʒ] ☐

c) ƎƏUAƏИƎ⅃ ☐

d) NUGAGELA ☐

2 Which words do you pronounce [hɪə]?

a) he ☐
b) her ☐
c) here ☐
d) hear ☐

3 Which phrase isn't correct?

a) How *much* flour is there? ☐
b) There's just *little* flour. ☐
c) How *many* cartons of milk do we need? ☐
d) We need just *a few* cartons. ☐

4 Which combination is wrong?

a) mid + night ☐
b) grand + parents ☐
c) disco + man ☐
d) web + site ☐

5 Complete the sentences. One verb doesn't fit.

drive • go • hurry • ride • run

a) Jack and Jane often ____________ shopping after school.
b) Do you know how to ____________ a unicycle?
c) ____________ up. School starts in five minutes.
d) Tim wants to ____________ his father's car when he's 17.

6 **Which two words don't rhyme?**

a) ten – then ☐
b) night – write ☐
c) can – fan ☐
d) hot – note ☐

Communication

7 **Read the German sentences and number the correct English translation. There's an example (0) for you.**

0	Wie wäre es, ins Kino zu gehen?
1	Wie spät ist es?
2	Was ist passiert?
3	Was hätten Sie gerne?
4	Was kann ich noch mit einem Handy machen?
5	Wie heißt dein Freund?

	What would you like?
0	What about going to the cinema?
	What happened?
	What's your friend's name?
	What else can I do with a mobile phone?
	What time is it?

Grammar

8 **Which form is correct?**

… you … a nice present for your last birthday, Teresa?

a) Don't … get ☐
b) Did … got ☐
c) Did … get ☐
d) Do … get ☐

9 Which short answer is correct?

Were you at the cinema last weekend, Brendan? – No, I …

a) weren't. ☐
b) didn't. ☐
c) wasn't. ☐
d) don't. ☐

10 Irregular verbs: Which form is wrong?

a) have – has – had ☐
b) take – took – taken ☐
c) send – sent – sent ☐
d) leave – left – left ☐

11 Use the correct word.

must • mustn't • need • needn't

a) Sorry, Aylin, but you ________________ use your mobile in the classroom.
b) When you go to the USA, you'll ________________ a digital photo.
c) You ________________ tidy your room. I can do that.
d) It's late. You ________________ go now.

12 Adverbs: Find the wrong form.

a) You can eat cheaply if you make your dinner at home. ☐
b) Mum always prepares our dinner very quickly. ☐
c) My brother sings rather beautifully. ☐
d) Jamie Oliver is famous because he cooks really good. ☐

Reading

Read this text. Then answer the questions.

FOUR TIPS TO KEEP FIT
- **Exercise outside three times a week for thirty minutes. Run or ride your bike.**
- **Eat fruit, salad and vegetables every day.**
- **Drink a lot of water every day. Don't drink too many sweet drinks. There's a lot of sugar in them.**
- **Don't forget breakfast. It's hard to start the day without a good breakfast. If you have breakfast every morning, you will have more energy and be successful in school.**

13 Which sentence is wrong?

a) Breakfast is very important for the whole day. ☐
b) Drinks which contain many sugar help you to feel good. ☐
c) Apples and carrots are better than chips and meat. ☐
d) Cycling and jogging help you to keep fit. ☐

14 Which statement is not in the text?

a) It's good to be active for about 90 minutes a week. ☐
b) You should drink a lot of milk. ☐
c) Breakfast helps you to be fitter and do better in school. ☐
d) You should eat salad every day. ☐

Culture

15 Complete the sentences. One word doesn't fit.

plays • music • November • Queen • French

a) Napoleon was ________________.
b) Mozart wrote famous ________________.
c) Elizabeth I was ________________ of England.
d) Guy Fawkes Day is in ________________ .

16 These countries are all English speaking countries except ...

a) Wales. ☐
b) Austria. ☐
c) Australia. ☐
d) Scotland. ☐

17 Which statement is wrong?

a) The language of pop music very often is English. ☐
b) The official language on ships and planes is English. ☐
c) One of the main languages on the Internet is English. ☐
d) People only speak English in Great Britain. ☐

Test 9

Vocabulary

1 **Which of these four examples doesn't show the word 'chocolate'?**

a) COCOLATHE ☐

b) ['tʃɒklət] ☐

c) ƎTA⅃OƆOHƆ ☐

d) TOOLASCHE ☐

2 **Which word do you pronounce [nəʊ]?**

a) no ☐
b) new ☐
c) now ☐
d) knew ☐

3 **Which is wrong?**

a) I don't have *many* things in my kitchen. ☐
b) There's *a little* sugar. ☐
c) And there are *a few* eggs. ☐
d) But there isn't *many* chocolate. ☐

4 **Which adjective is wrong?**

a) sun – sunny ☐
b) fog – foggy ☐
c) rain – rainny ☐
d) cloud – cloudy ☐

5 **Complete the sentences. One word doesn't fit.**

leave • life • live • lives • love

a) Where do you ________________? – At 15 King's Road.
b) Tyson said 'Goodbye' because he wanted to ________________ .
c) Grandpa Ken had a very hard ________________.
d) I ________________ the T-shirt you're wearing today.

6 **Which two words don't rhyme?**

a) at - that ☐
b) pet - get ☐
c) although - through ☐
d) sun - done ☐

Communication

7 **Read the German sentences and number the correct English translations. There's an example (0) for you. One sentence doesn't fit.**

0	Welches Computerspiel magst du?
1	Wann beginnt das Spiel?
2	Woher kommst du?
3	Wer ist der Junge?
4	Wessen Computerspiel ist das?
5	Warum weinst du?

	Whose computer game is this?
	Who's the boy?
0	Which computer game do you like?
	Where is the boy?
	When does the game begin?
	Why are you crying?
	Where are you from?

Grammar

8 **Which comparison is wrong?**

a) nice - nicer - (the) nicest ☐
b) big - bigger - (the) biggest ☐
c) busy - busyer - (the) busyest ☐
d) hot - hotter - (the) hottest ☐

9 **Irregular forms of comparison. Which is correct?**

a) bad – worse – (the) worsest ☐
b) good – besser – (the) best ☐
c) bad – worse – (the) worst ☐
d) good – better – (the) besst ☐

10 **Comparisons. Find the mistake.**

a) One T-shirt is cheap, but two belts are cheaper. ☐
b) The handbag is the most expensive thing here. ☐
c) Let's buy the T-shirt, it is more nice. ☐
d) The T-shirt is expensive, the handbag is more expensive. ☐

11 **Which comparison is wrong?**

I think that …

a) Hyde Park is *the most beautiful park* in London. ☐
b) London policemen are *the most politest* in England. ☐
c) London Dungeon is *more exciting than* the London Eye. ☐
d) Tower of London is *more famous than* the Beefeaters. ☐

12 **going to-future: Which sentence doesn't express a plan?**

a) Look, the girls are going to school. ☐
b) Shelly is going to visit her boyfriend. ☐
c) We're going to go to the zoo on Sunday. ☐
d) Aaron: I'm going to watch Chelsea – Manchester next Saturday. ☐

Reading

Read this ad. Then answer the questions.

BIG MODERN FLAT

WITH A LIVING ROOM, TWO BEDROOMS, KITCHEN AND ONE BATHROOM

Good, quiet location near Greenwich Park • Nice garden with a small terrace • Private garage • 7 minutes from bus station
Rent: £ 260 per week

telephone: 020-7431-4768 • mobile: 07787-9561450

13 **Which statement is wrong?**

a) There are five rooms in the flat. ☐
b) The street in front of the flat isn't very noisy. ☐
c) The flat costs less than £ 1,000 per month. ☐
d) The price includes a garage and a garden with a terrace. ☐

14 **What does this sign mean? Tick (✓) the right answer.**

a) You have to pay if you park your bike here. ☐
b) You mustn't park your bike here. ☐
c) You can ride your bike here. ☐
d) You can park your bike here. ☐

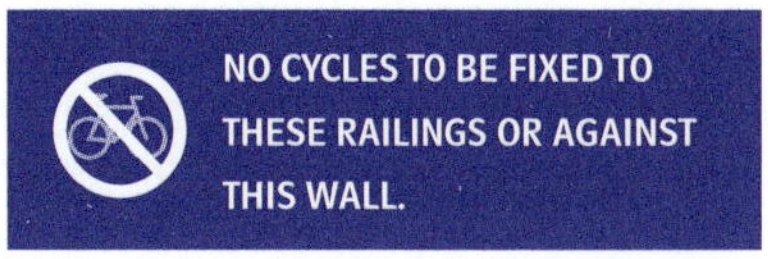

Culture

15 **Prince Charles' family name is ...**

a) Wimbledon. ☐
b) Buckingham. ☐
c) Windsor. ☐
d) Oxford. ☐

16 **Prince William, the Queen's grandson, is married to ...**

a) Diana Spencer. ☐
b) Maid Marian. ☐
c) Camilla Parker Bowles. ☐
d) Kate Middleton. ☐

17 **The first line of the British National Anthem* is:**

a) 'Our Queen is the greatest'. ☐
b) 'Britain for ever'. ☐
c) 'God save our gracious Queen'. ☐
d) 'We praise** our Queen'. ☐

*Nationalhymne **loben, preisen

Vocabulary

1 Which of these four examples show the word 'embarrassing'?

a) AABEGIRRSSMN ☐

b) [ɪm'bærəsɪŋ] ☐

c) ƏИIƧAЯAᗺMƎ ☐

d) MASRRINAGBEA ☐

2 Which words do you pronounce [ðeə]?

a) the ☐
b) their ☐
c) they ☐
d) there ☐

3 Which is correct?

a) three bar of chocolate ☐
b) two bags sugar ☐
c) four cartons of milk ☐
d) two bottles water ☐

4 Which pair doesn't fit?

a) long – short ☐
b) good – bad ☐
c) different – (the) same ☐
d) cheap – cheaper ☐

5 Complete the sentences. One verb doesn't fit.

hear • listen • look at • see • watch

a) We want to ______________ the football game on TV.
b) Did you ______________ that noise?
c) It was too dark to ______________ anything.
d) Do you often ______________ to hard rock music?

6 **Which two words don't rhyme?**

a) blue - new ☐
b) good - should ☐
c) hope - shop ☐
d) four - more ☐

Communication

7 **Read the German sentences and number the correct English translations. There's an example (0) for you. One sentence doesn't fit.**

0	Entschuldigen Sie, wo ist das Kino?
1	Gehen Sie geradeaus.
2	Biegen Sie rechts ab.
3	Gehen Sie an der Zoohandlung vorbei.
4	Überqueren Sie den Marktplatz.
5	Biegen Sie an der nächsten Ampel links ab.
6	Das Kino ist gegenüber vom Bahnhof, zwischen der Buchhandlung und der Post.

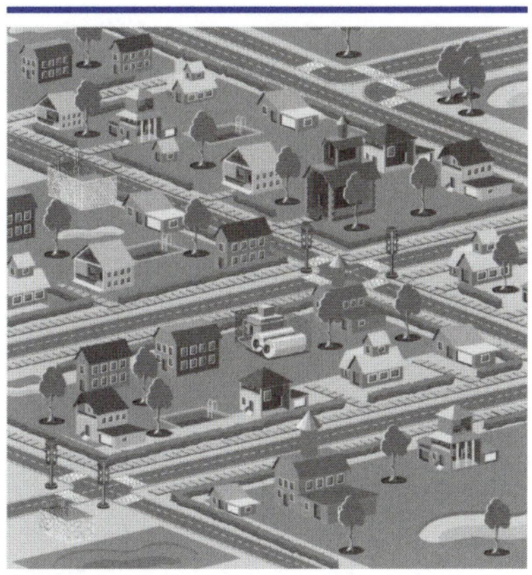

	Go past the pet shop.
0	Excuse me, where is the cinema?
	Turn right.
	The cinema is at the corner.
	Turn left at the next traffic lights.
	The cinema is opposite the station, between the bookshop and the post office.
	Cross the market square.
	Go straight on.

Grammar

8 **Which word is usually not used with the present perfect?**

a) ever ☐
b) ago ☐
c) never ☐
d) not yet ☐

9 **Which form of the present perfect is wrong?**

a) Have you ever seen the film 'Robin Hood'? ☐
b) Kevin has never played the Sheriff of Nottingham. ☐
c) Has Mandy ever heared of Maid Marian and Friar Tuck? ☐
d) Some pupils haven't read the story of Robin Hood and Little John yet. ☐

10 **Simple past or present perfect: Which sentence is wrong?**

a) I have already told Carol about the fantastic new Science Fiction film. ☐
b) My friends and I have watched it last weekend. ☐
c) I read the story about the aliens some months ago. ☐
d) Carol has not read the book yet. ☐

11 **Which 'if clause' is wrong?**

a) If our computer breaks down, we'll see what's wrong. ☐
b) If you try again, maybe it'll work. ☐
c) I am happy if I get a new mobile for my birthday. ☐
d) If you don't come home at the right time, we'll call the police. ☐

Reading

Read this e-mail. Then answer the questions.

FIONA HEARN, 13, FEMALE, UNITED KINGDOM	WRITING LANGUAGE: ENGLISH

I am looking for pen friends all over the world. My interests are reading (mainly short stories and poetry), writing letters, computers, films, art (I paint) and animals. We have three cats. I also make greetings cards. My family live near Dundee/Scotland and I go to John's Secondary School in Dundee. I have a good sense of humour. I would love to hear from anyone around my own age, please, who would like a pen friend in Scotland.
Best wishes
Fiona

12 **Which statement is wrong?**

Fiona …

a) likes writing short stories and poetry. ☐
b) paints in her free time. ☐
c) has got some pets. ☐
d) likes watching films. ☐

13 **Which statement is not in the text?**

Fiona …

a) goes to school in Scotland. ☐
b) enjoys a good laugh. ☐
c) is looking for a pen friend who is about thirteen years old. ☐
d) wants a pen friend in Europe only. ☐

Culture

14 **Which statement is wrong?**

a) Whitney Houston was a singer. ☐
b) Guy Fawkes was a king. ☐
c) The Beatles were a famous band. ☐
d) Robin Hood was a hero*. ☐

* Held

15 **Which town is famous for Robin Hood?**

a) Manchester ☐
b) Liverpool ☐
c) Nottingham ☐
d) London ☐

16 **Which statement is wrong?**

All schools in England have an 'Open Day'. That means that pupils …

a) present their school life. ☐
b) act out plays. ☐
c) go on a school trip. ☐
d) have some sports competitions. ☐

Lösungen

Test 1

Vocabulary

1: d) = 1, a) = 2, b) = 3, c) = 4; 2 b) Tuesday; 3 b); 4 c); 5 a) ride b) do c) play d) read; 6 c)

Communication

7a) +, b) +, c) –, d) +; 8: b) = 1, d) = 2, a) = 3, c) = 4

Grammar

9 c); 10 d); 11 a) your b) my c) their d) our; 12 d)

Reading

13: c) = 1, a) = 2, d) = 3, b) = 4; 14 b)

Culture

15 b); 16 b), d); 17 a)

Test 2

Vocabulary

1: d) = 1, a) = 2, c) = 3, b) = 4; 2 c); 3 a); 4 b); 5 a) take b) put c) do d) make; 6 a)

Communication

7 c); 8: c) = 1, a) = 2, d) = 3, b) = 4

Grammar

9 b); 10 b); 11 a) her b) them c) him d) me; 12 c)

Reading

13: c) = 1, d) = 2, a) = 3, b) = 4; 14 b)

Culture

15 c); 16 a); 17 b)

Test 3

Vocabulary

1: d) = 1, a) = 2, c) = 3, b) = 4; 2 c); 3 b); 4 a); 5 a) tell b) spell c) say d) speak; 6 b)

Communication

7 a) +, b) –, c) +, d) +; 8 b)

Grammar

9 c); 10 c); 11 d); 12 a)

Reading

13 c); 14 c)

Culture

15 d); 16 c); 17 b)

Test 4

Vocabulary

1: d) = 1, b) = 2, c) = 3, a) = 4; 2 c); 3 b); 4 b); 5 a) call b) shout c) cry d) Ask; 6 a)

Communication

7: b) = 1, d) = 2, a) = 3, c) = 4; 8 a) Excuse b) not far c) get d) straight

Grammar

9 a); 10 c); 11 d); 12 c)

Reading

13 c); 14 d)

Culture

15 b); 16 c); 17 c)

Test 5

Vocabulary

1: b) = 1, c) = 2, d) = 3, a) = 4; 2 a) write b) talk c) listen d) knife; 3 b); 4 c); 5 a) carry b) wear c) bring d) take; 6c)

Communication

7: b) = 1, d) = 2, a) = 3, c) = 4; 8 a) for b) because c) or d) instead of

Grammar

9 a); 10 c); 11 a); 12 b)

Reading

13 a); 14 c)

Culture
15 c); 16 c); 17 b), c)

Test 6

Vocabulary
1 d); 2 a) climb b) know c) walk d) wrong; 3 b); 4 c); 5 a) because b) or c) although d) also; 6 b)

Communication
7

5	How about Friday at 7?
3	How much must I pay?
6	How much are the postcards?
2	Where are you from?
0	How old are you?
4	How many CDs do you have?
1	How are you?

Grammar
8 b); 9 a) isn't b) 's c) 'm d) 're; 10 a) Who b) What c) How d) Where; 11 b); 12 b)

Reading
13 c); 14 a)

Culture
15 b); 16 c); 17 d)

Test 7

Vocabulary
1 d); 2 a), c); 3 c); 4 a); 5 b)

Communication
6

4	Where is it often sunny and hot?
6	I love the month of May.
5	Which month don't you like?
2	What's your favourite season?
1	What's the weather like today?
0	How old are you?
3	It's raining everywhere today.

Grammar
7 a); 8 d); 9 b); 10 a); 11 d)

Reading
12 b); 13 c)

Culture
14 b); 15 b); 16 b)

Test 8

Vocabulary
1 c); 2 c), d); 3 b); 4 c); 5 a) go b) ride c) Hurry d) drive; 6 d)

Communication
7

3	What would you like?
0	What about going to the cinema?
2	What happened?
5	What's your friend's name?
4	What else can I do with a mobile phone?
1	What time is it?

Grammar
8 c); 9 c); 10 a); 11 a) mustn't b) need c) needn't d) must; 12 d)

Reading
13 b); 14 b)

Culture
15a) French b) music c) Queen d) November;
16b); 17d)

Test 9

Vocabulary
1d); 2d); 3d); 4c); 5a) live b) leave c) life d) love;
6c)

Communication
7

4	Whose computer game is this?
3	Who's the boy?
0	Which computer game do you like?
–	Where is the boy?
1	When does the game begin?
5	Why are you crying?
2	Where are you from?

Grammar
8c); 9c); 10c); 11b); 12a)

Reading
13c); 14b)

Culture
15c); 16d); 17c)

Test 10

Vocabulary
1a, b); 2b, d); 3c); 4d); 5a) watch b) hear c) see
d) listen; 6c)

Communication
7

3	Go past the pet shop.
0	Excuse me, where is the cinema?
2	Turn right.
–	The cinema is at the corner.
5	Turn left at the next traffic lights.
6	The cinema is opposite the station, between the bookshop and the post office.
4	Cross the market square.
1	Go straight on.

Grammar
8b); 9c); 10b); 11c)

Reading
12a); 13d)

Culture
14b); 15c); 16c)

Your test report

Tip 1: Always mark your answers with a pencil so that you can do the tasks again.
Tip 2: Check your answers on pages 44 – 46.
Tip 3: Count your right answers and make a cross in the table below.
Tip 4: Read the comment on your result on the next page.

Right answers:	**14 – 17**	**11 – 13**	**8 – 10**	**4 – 7**	**0 – 3**
Test 1					
Test 2					
Test 3					
Test 4					
Test 5					
Test 6					
Test 7					
Test 8					
Test 9					
Test 10					

Comment on your test result

14–17 right answers:	**Excellent!**	You did very well! Go on to the next test.
11–13 right answers:	**Good!**	Mark your wrong answers with a coloured pencil. Do these tasks again after two or three days. Look up the difficult words in a dictionary.
8–10 right answers:	**Satisfactory!**	Look at the wrong tasks again. Do half of these tasks the next day, repeat until all answers are correct. Look up the difficult words in a dictionary. Do some grammar revision.
4–7 right answers:	**You can do better!**	Think positive, but you have to do more to get a better mark. Learn some English words every day. Write ten words on cards every day and learn them. Do more grammar revision.
0–3 right answers:	**No comment!**	Are you sure that you tried hard?

- 10 Standard-Tests zur Erweiterung der sprachlichen Kompetenzen
- Systematisches Üben zum Ankreuzen mit Multiple-Choice
- Jeder Test in 15 Minuten lösbar
- Selbstauswertungs- und Lösungsteil

ISBN 978-3-12-547487-1
9 783125 474871